THIS BOOK BELONGS TO:

_____

_____

_____

AGE _____

Follow "Little Worm Books" on Amazon to stay updated on new books and giveaways! Or email us at littlewormbooks@gmail.com

JOIN OUR MAILING LIST AND GAIN ACCESS TO HUNDREDS OF FREE COLORING PAGE PRINTOUTS!

UNLOCK YOUR PHONE AND OPEN THE CAMERA FOR THE LINK!

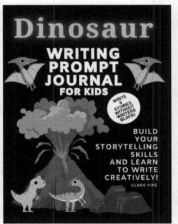

Copyright © 2024 Little Worm Books

STEP-BY-STEP STORYTELLING
For Kids

A CHILD'S CREATIVE WRITING GUIDE FOR CRAFTING COMPLETE STORIES!

CLARA VINE

Table of Contents

Introduction

Welcome to Your Writing Adventure!

You're about to start a fantastic journey into the world of writing. Remember, every great writer started just like you, with a blank page and a head full of ideas. Don't worry if your first stories aren't perfect. Writing is like a secret path full of twists and turns. Sometimes, you'll sprint ahead; other times, you might take a few steps back or even have to start over. That's all part of the process!

Think of your favorite stories and songs. Even the best writers and musicians started with a simple idea and grew it into something extraordinary. They practiced, made mistakes, learned, and kept going. And now it's your turn to do the same.

In this book, you'll find all kinds of writing prompts – little sparks to ignite your imagination. Each one is a new world waiting for you to explore. Don't be afraid to try something different to make your stories uniquely yours.

As you write, remember that every word you put down is a step forward on your journey. You'll learn new things, improve your skills, and, most importantly, have fun! There's no right or wrong way to tell your story – it's all about expressing who you are and your unique ideas.

So, grab your pen, open your heart to adventure, and let's start writing.

In the writing world, anything is possible – all you need to do is begin! Happy writing, and enjoy the journey!

CHAPTER 1

Parts of Speech and Sentence Structure

Parts of Speech

Parts of speech are like different categories of words in the English Language. Each category has its own job in a sentence. There are nouns for naming things, pronouns for replacing nouns, verbs for action or being, adjectives for describing things, adverbs for adding detail to actions or descriptions, prepositions for showing relationships between words, conjunctions for joining words or sentences, interjections for showing strong feelings, and articles for pointing out specific or general things. Understanding these helps you put words together correctly to make sentences.

- Nouns
- Pronouns
- Verbs
- Adjectives
- Adverbs
- Prepositions
- Conjunctions
- Interjections
- Articles

<u>Nouns</u>: Nouns are the names of things, places, people, or ideas. They are like labels we put on everything around us. For example, 'dog,' 'school,' 'teacher,' and 'map' are all nouns. Nouns can be something you can touch, like a 'ball,' or something you can't, like 'bravery.'

<u>Examples</u>:
Adventure, Mountain, Ocean, Forest, River, City, Garden, Playground, School, Library, Book, Toy, Animal, Bird, Fish, Insect, Flower, Tree, Fruit, Vegetable, Food, Dessert, Cake, Candy, Ice cream, Drink, Water, Juice, Milk, Tea, Coffee, Sun, Moon, Star, Sky, Cloud, Rain, Snow, Wind, Storm, Car, Bus, Train, Bicycle, Airplane, Boat, Road, Bridge, Path, and Building.

Write and draw some of your favorite nouns!-

<u>Verbs</u>: Verbs are action words. They tell us what something or someone is doing. If you're running, jumping, thinking, or dreaming, those are all actions, so they are verbs. Verbs make things happen in a sentence. An example sentence is, "The dog barked loudly at the mailman." In this sentence, "barked" is the verb. It describes the action that the dog is performing. The verb "barked" tells us what the dog is doing, which is the central action in this sentence.

<u>Examples</u>: Run, Jump, Laugh, Sing, Dance, Think, Swim, Fly, Write, Draw, Read, Play, Whisper, Climb, Explore, Build, Cook, Paint, Search, Travel, Discover, Invent, Create, Listen, Watch, Dream, Chase, Hide, Seek, Grow, Learn, Teach, Skate, Slide, Dive, Wave, Cheer, Shout, Imagine, Remember, Forget, Solve, Stretch, Bend, Spin, Twirl, Kick, Roll, Push, and Pull.

Write and draw some of your favorite verbs!-

Adjectives: Adjectives describe nouns. They give us more information about a thing, a place, a person, or an idea. For example, 'blue sky,' 'loud music,' 'happy child,' and 'spicy food.' Adjectives help us picture things more clearly in our minds. An example sentence is, "The bright sun warmed the sandy beach." In this sentence, "bright" is the adjective. It describes the noun "sun," giving us more information about its quality or appearance. The adjective "bright" helps create a vivid image of the sun, emphasizing its intensity and how it illuminates the beach.

Examples: Happy, Sad, Bright, Dark, Large, Small, Soft, Hard, Sweet, Bitter, Loud, Quiet, Tall, Short, Long, Young, Old, Fast, Slow, Strong, Weak, Funny, Serious, Beautiful, Ugly, Clean, Dirty, Rich, Poor, Heavy, Light, Full, Empty, Thick, Thin, Smooth, Rough, Wet, Dry, Fresh, Stale, Bright, Colorful, Plain, Fancy, Simple, Elegant, Round, Square, and Flat.

Write and draw some of your favorite adjectives!-

Adverbs: Adverbs usually describe verbs but can also describe adjectives or other adverbs. They tell us how, when, where, or how often something is done. For instance, 'quickly run,' 'very small,' 'happily sing,' or 'often visit.' Adverbs add more detail to actions and descriptions. An example sentence is, "The cat quietly sneaked into the room." In this sentence, "quietly" is the adverb. It modifies the verb "sneaked," telling us how the cat sneaked into the room. The adverb "quietly" adds detail to the action, indicating that it was done silently or gently.

Examples: Quickly, Slowly, Loudly, Quietly, Happily, Sadly, Easily, Hardly, Brightly, Gently, Roughly, Suddenly, Usually, Often, Rarely, Nearly, Really, Simply, Carefully, Carelessly, Eagerly, Gracefully, Awkwardly, Always, Never, Sometimes, Frequently, Occasionally, Constantly, Regularly, Seldom, Immediately, Instantly, Briefly.

Write and draw some of your favorite adverbs!-

Pronouns: Pronouns are words that replace nouns. Instead of repeating a noun repeatedly, you can use pronouns like 'he,' 'she,' 'it,' 'they,' 'you,' 'we,' 'his,' 'her,' and 'there.' For example, instead of saying 'Maria likes Maria's bike,' you say 'Maria likes her bike.'

Examples: I, You, He, She, It, We, They, Me, Him, Her, Us, Them, My, Your, His, Her, Its, Our, Their, Mine, Yours, His, Hers, Ours, Theirs, Myself, Yourself, Himself, Herself, Itself, Ourselves, Yourselves, Themselves, Who, Whom, Whose, Whoever, and Whomever.

Prepositions: Prepositions show the relationship of a noun or a pronoun to another word in the sentence. They can indicate time, place, or other types of relationships. Examples include 'in,' 'on,' 'at,' 'by,' 'for,' 'with,' 'about,' 'under,' 'over,' and 'between.' An example sentence is, "The cat slept under the table." In this sentence, "under" is the preposition. It is used to show the relationship between the noun "table" and the action of the cat sleeping. The preposition "under" tells us where the cat is in relation to the table, indicating that the cat is beneath it.

Examples: In, On, At, By, For, With, About, Against, Among, Between, Over, Under, Beside, Around, Before, After, During, Through, Into, Out, Off, Above, Below, Beyond, Near, Far, Inside, Outside, Onto, To, From, Up, Down, Across, Along, Past, Toward, Within, Without, Beneath, Underneath, Amongst, Alongside, Amid, Amidst, Opposite

Interjections: Interjections are words that express emotion. They are often used at the beginning of a sentence and can stand alone. Examples include 'Wow!', 'Oops!', 'Hurray!' and 'Oh no!'. They help convey feelings in our speech and writing.

Examples: Wow!, Oops!, Yay!, Aha!, Alas!, Hey!, Oh!, Ouch!, Hooray!, Eek!, Uh-oh!, Hmmm., Yikes!, Whoa!, Ahem., Shh!, Phew!, Yippee!, Aww., Bah!, Bravo!, Eureka!, Gosh!, Ha!, Hurrah!, Mmm., Nah., Psst!, Gee., Ugh!, Well., Yum!, Zap!, Blah., Boo!, Duh!, Huh?, Meh., Pff., Sigh., Ack!, Brr!, Ew!, Gulp!, Hmm., Oopsie!, Tsk-tsk., Woof!, Yowza!, Zing!

Conjunctions: Conjunctions join words, phrases, or clauses in a sentence. They help make our sentences more complex and connected. Some common conjunctions are 'and,' 'but,' 'or,' 'so,' and 'because.' For example, 'I wanted to play, but it was raining'.

Examples: And, But, Or, Nor, Because, Unless, Although, Though, While, When, If, Whereas, Whether, Even if, Even though, Now that, Provided that, Seeing that, So that, In order that, As long as, As soon as, As much as, No sooner than

Write and draw some of your favorite pronouns, prepositions, interjections and conjunctions!

"Do what you can, with what you have, where you are."
- Theodore Roosevelt

"Nothing is impossible. The word itself says 'I'm possible!'"
- Audrey Hepburn

9

Articles: Articles are just these three small words: 'the,' 'a,' and 'an.' The purpose of an article is to clarify who or what you're talking about in a sentence.

Example Sentence: "The cat sat on a mat." This sentence has two articles: "The" and "a."

"The" is used before "cat." It is a definite article, which means it points to a specific cat that both the speaker and listener know. It's like saying, "I am talking about THIS specific cat, not another cat."

"A" is used before "mat." It is an indefinite article, which means it refers to any mat, not a specific one. It's used when the exact identity of the mat is not known or not necessary.

In summary, the article "the" specifies a particular cat, while "a" introduces a new, non-specific item (mat) into the sentence.

Write your own sentence and circle the articles-

10

How To Write a Sentence

Now that you know the essential parts of speech in the English Language, it is time to put it all together. So, what makes a good sentence?

Every sentence needs at least two critical parts of speech to be complete:

Noun (or Pronoun): This is the sentence's subject, which can be a person, place, thing, or idea. It tells us what or who the sentence is about.

Verb: This shows the action or state of being. The verb tells us what the subject is doing or being.

For example, in the sentence "The dog barks," 'dog' is the noun (subject), and 'barks' is the verb (action).

Some sentences might use a pronoun (like 'he,' 'she,' 'it,' or 'they') instead of a noun for the subject. For example, "She sings." Here, 'She' is the Pronoun, and 'sings' is the verb.

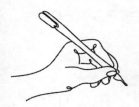 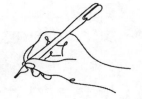

Tips for Writing Sentences

Clear and Complete: A good sentence should have a clear subject (such as a person or thing) and a verb (the action). For example, "The cat sleeps." This way, your sentence conveys a complete idea.

Just the Right Length: Your sentence shouldn't be too long or too short. Long sentences can be confusing, and short ones might not tell enough. But sometimes, a brief sentence can be powerful!

Descriptive: Using adjectives (describing words) and adverbs (words that describe how something is done) makes your sentence more interesting. For instance, "The fluffy cat sleeps quietly."

Makes Sense on Its Own: A good sentence should make sense on its own without requiring extra information from the rest of the paragraph.

Fits Well with Others: It should connect smoothly with the sentences around it, helping to build your story or explanation.

Correct Grammar and Punctuation: Using grammar and punctuation correctly makes your sentence easy to understand. It's like following rules in a game.

Shows Your Style: The best sentences show your unique style, whether serious, funny, formal, or casual.

Varied Starters: Mixing up how you start your sentences keeps your writing interesting.

Clear and Exact: Good sentences are straightforward, and use precise words to share your ideas.

Matches the Tone: Your sentence should match the feel of your story or explanation, whether serious, playful, or something else.

Engaging and Interesting: Great sentences grab readers' attention with cool facts or vivid descriptions.

All these tips work together to help you write sentences that are fun to read and get your ideas across clearly. Remember, the more you practice writing and read different books, the better you'll get at making awesome sentences!

What tip did you find most helpful?-

Sentence Examples-

Sentence 1: "The playful kitten chased the rolling ball across the sunny garden."

The - Article
playful - Adjective
kitten - Noun (subject)
chased - Verb (action)
the - Article
rolling - Adjective
ball - Noun (object)
across - Preposition
the - Article
sunny - Adjective
garden - Noun (object of the preposition)

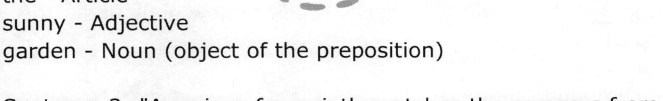

Sentence 2: "A curious fox quietly watches the campers from behind a tree."

A - Article
curious - Adjective
fox - Noun (subject)
quietly - Adverb
watches - Verb (action)
the - Article
campers - Noun (object)
from - Preposition
behind - Preposition
a - Article
tree - Noun (object of the preposition)

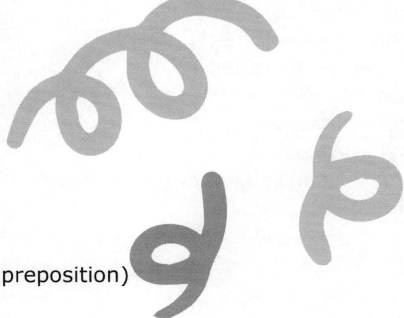

Sentence 3: "During the summer, we often go swimming in the lake."

During - Preposition
the - Article
summer - Noun (object of the preposition)
we - Pronoun (subject)
often - Adverb
go - Verb (action)
swimming - Verb (gerund)
in - Preposition
the - Article
lake - Noun (object of the preposition)

Sentence 4: "She enthusiastically read her new book under the old oak tree."

She - Pronoun (subject)
enthusiastically - Adverb
read - Verb (action)
her - Possessive pronoun
new - Adjective
book - Noun (object)
under - Preposition
the - Article
old - Adjective
oak - Adjective
tree - Noun (object of the preposition)

Sentence 5: "The teacher asked a difficult question, and the students thought hard."

The - Article
teacher - Noun (subject)
asked - Verb (action)
a - Article
difficult - Adjective
question - Noun (object)
and - Conjunction
the - Article
students - Noun (subject)
thought - Verb (action)
hard - Adverb

Sentence 6: "In the bright morning light, colorful birds sang cheerfully."

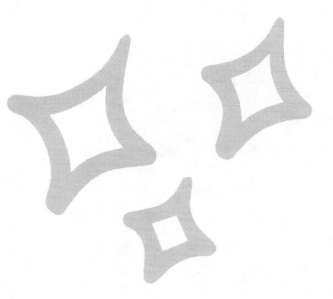

In - Preposition
the - Article
bright - Adjective
morning - Noun (object of the preposition)
light - Noun
colorful - Adjective
birds - Noun (subject)
sang - Verb (action)
cheerfully - Adverb

Use this section to write practice sentences. Make a list of the parts of speech in each sentence.

"Shoot for the moon. Even if you miss, you'll land among the stars."

- Norman Vincent Peale

"The secret of getting ahead is getting started."

- Mark Twain

CHAPTER 2

Building Blocks All Writers Need

How to Become an Excellent Writer

<u>Read a Lot</u>: Reading is a secret ingredient for becoming a great writer. When you read, you learn new words, see how stories come together, and get many fantastic ideas.

<u>Write Regularly</u>: Practice makes perfect! Try to write every day, even a little bit. It could be a story, a diary entry, or even just a few sentences about your day. The more you write, the better you'll get.

<u>Use Your Imagination</u>: Let your imagination go wild! Think of the craziest, most interesting, or funniest ideas. Your imagination makes your writing unique and special.

<u>Learn New Words</u>: A good writer knows lots of words. Reading helps with this, and you can also use a dictionary or a thesaurus to learn new words to make your writing more interesting.

<u>Ask for Feedback</u>: Share your writing with friends, family, or teachers and ask what they think. Don't be afraid of criticism – it helps you improve. Even professional writers have editors! Sometimes, it is tough to see the flaws in our writing. Don't let it discourage you!

<u>Edit Your Work</u>: After writing something, go back and read it again and again. Look for mistakes or areas where you can improve your writing. Editing is an essential part of writing.

<u>Have Fun with It</u>: Writing should be fun! Write about things you love or find interesting. Enjoy the process of creating your own stories, characters, and worlds.

<u>Study Writing</u>: Pay attention in your English or writing classes at school. They teach you lots of valuable things about how to write well.

<u>Be Patient</u>: Becoming a good writer takes time. Don't worry if it seems hard at first. Every writer improves over time with practice.

<u>Keep a Journal or Idea Book</u>: This can be a special place to write down ideas, thoughts, or things you notice. Sometimes, these small ideas can turn into big stories.

Remember, every writer started somewhere!

 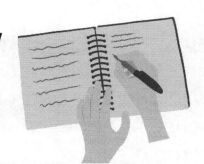

Why Write?

Writing is a superpower with countless benefits. Here are a few-

<u>Share Your Stories</u>: You can create your worlds and characters, like being a movie director in your head!

<u>Express Feelings</u>: If you're happy, sad, excited, or even angry, writing helps you share those feelings. It's like talking to a friend who always listens.

<u>Boost Your Mood</u>: Writing about happy moments or things you're thankful for can make you even happier.

Be Creative: You get to use your imagination and come up with all sorts of fun ideas.

Remember Things Better: Writing down things, like what you did on your summer vacation, helps you remember them later.

Become Smarter: Writing helps you learn new words and improve grammar, making all your homework easier!

Solve Problems: When you have a problem, writing it down can help you solve it. Putting your problem into words on paper or on a computer is like looking at it in a new way, not just thinking about it in your head. Writing it down can help you understand your thoughts and help you figure out what to do next.

Build Confidence: Writing a good story is a journey that takes time and effort and is usually challenging. But reaching the end is incredibly rewarding. When you complete your story, the sense of achievement is exciting, making you proud to have completed it.

Relax and Have Fun: Writing can be a fantastic hobby, like drawing or playing games. It's fun and can help you relax.

Connect with Others: You can share your writing with friends or family and connect with people who like the same things as you. It can also help you express yourself to loved ones when you feel emotions about another person or situation.

So, whether it's telling exciting stories, sharing your feelings, or having fun, writing is a great way to express yourself and grow!

Elements of a Good Story

Characters: Your story's people, animals, or even magical creatures. Good characters are exciting and make you want to know more about them. They can be brave, funny, smart, or even break the rules. You should feel excited to see what they will do next.

Setting: This is where and when your story happens. It could be a jungle adventure in the past, a mystery in a modern city, or a journey in space in the future. The setting helps you imagine you're right there in the story.

Plot: This is what happens in the story. A good plot has exciting events like a problem that must be solved, a journey to a new place, or a challenge the characters must overcome. It keeps you turning the pages to see what happens next.

Conflict: This is a big problem or challenge in the story. It could be a dragon that needs to be defeated, a mystery that needs to be solved, or a race to find a hidden treasure. The conflict makes the story exciting and keeps you guessing what will happen.

Resolution: This is how the problem or conflict in the story gets solved. It's often towards the end of the story. A suitable resolution makes you happy or satisfied because everything works out in the end, even if it's not how you expected.

Elements of a Plot

A good plot is essential in a story, especially for keeping it exciting and fun to read. Here are elements that make a good plot-

Interesting and Clear: A good plot in a story is easy to understand and full of cool stuff happening. It's like a treasure hunt where each clue leads you to the next exciting spot, and you always know how to find what's next.

Exciting Problem or Challenge: Every good plot has a problem or challenge the characters must solve. The problem could be anything from finding a hidden treasure, saving a magical world, or solving a mystery. It keeps you wondering what will happen next.

Twists and Turns: Just like a game with unexpected moves, a good plot has surprises that make you say, "Wow!" or "I didn't see that coming!" It could be a secret revealed, a sudden change of plans, or a character who isn't who they seem to be.

Characters Grow and Change: In a good plot, the characters learn something or change somehow. Maybe they become braver, kinder, or understand something important about themselves. It makes the story more meaningful.

<u>Build-Up and Problem-Solving</u>: A good plot builds up excitement or tension and then cleverly solves the problem. The ending should answer most questions and tie up the story neatly.

<u>Makes You Feel Emotions</u>: A good plot makes you feel things - happy, sad, excited, or even a bit scared. It's like a rollercoaster with ups and downs that make the ride fun.

<u>Engages Your Imagination</u>: A good plot makes you imagine the scenes like a movie. You can picture the characters, the places, and the action as if you're in the story.

Remember, a good plot keeps you turning the pages because you want to know what happens next. It's the heart of a great story!

 # Who, What, When, Where, Why?

In every good story, you discover who it's about, what's happening, when and where, and why everything is happening. It helps make the story exciting and lets you picture everything in your mind like you're there!

<u>Who</u>: Think about the characters in your story. 'Who' are they? They could be anyone you imagine - like a daring space explorer, a crafty wizard, or even a dinosaur who loves to dance! Your characters are the stars of your story.

<u>What</u>: This is about your story's adventure or main action in the story. 'What' is happening to your characters? Are they going on a secret mission, discovering a hidden world, or solving a tricky puzzle? 'What' makes your story full of action and thrills!

<u>When</u>: You need to decide the time of your story. Is it set in a long, long time ago, in the days of dinosaurs? Or maybe far in the future, where people live on different planets? It is very important to describe 'when' your story is!

<u>Where</u>: 'Where' is your story set? It's all about the location. It could be in a mysterious jungle, a bustling city, or even in a magical land above the clouds! 'Where' creates the special world where your story happens.

<u>Why</u>: This is about the reason behind everything in your story. Why is the hero on a quest? Why did the mysterious spaceship land in your backyard? 'Why' adds depth and mystery to your story, making it really intriguing.

· · · · · · ● ● ● ● ● ● ● · · ·

When you're ready to write your story, remember these five Ws. They're your guide to creating a complete story that anyone will want to read twice!

· · · · · · ● ● ● ● ● ● · · ·

Elements of a Paragraph

A good paragraph is an essential part of writing, whether it's a story or an essay. Here's how you can craft a strong paragraph-

<u>Start with a Main Idea</u>: Your paragraph should begin with a topic sentence that introduces the central idea. This sentence sets the stage for the rest of the paragraph's discussion.

<u>Add Supporting Details</u>: After your topic sentence, add more details, examples, or explanations. These additional sentences reinforce and clarify your main idea, providing a fuller, more complete understanding of the topic you're discussing.

<u>Keep it Clear and Organized</u>: Arrange your sentences in a logical order. This helps your reader easily understand and follow your ideas.

<u>Use Transitions</u>: Transition words or phrases are essential to connect your ideas smoothly, guiding your reader from one thought to the next.

<u>Conclude Well</u>: A good paragraph often ends with a concluding sentence summarizing the main idea or adding a final insight. This is a way to neatly tie up your thoughts.

<u>Vary Your Sentence Structure</u>: Mix up short and long sentences or different types of sentences to keep your paragraph engaging and dynamic.

Be Descriptive and Engaging: Use descriptive words to paint a vivid picture in your reader's mind. It makes your writing more exciting and lively.

Use Correct Grammar and Punctuation: Proper grammar and punctuation are necessary for making your paragraph clear and easy to read.

Writing a great paragraph is like creating a team where each sentence works together to present a single idea clearly and interestingly. Practice regularly, and remember to have fun with your writing!

Writing
Tip Sheet

Writer's block got you down? Would you like any help knowing what to write next? Here are some tips!-

Start with the Five Ws: If you're stuck, think about the 'Who,' 'What,' 'When,' 'Where,' and 'Why' of your story. Who is your character? What is happening? When and where is it taking place? Why is it happening?

You can imagine the Setting: Think about where your story happens. Is it in a forest, a city, or another planet? Visualize it and describe what you see.

Create Interesting Characters: Develop your characters. What do they look like? What are their personalities? What do they like and dislike?

Add Dialogue: Have your characters talk to each other. Dialogue can move the story forward and show your characters' personalities.

Build a Problem: Every good story has a problem or challenge. What does your character want or need? What's stopping them from getting it?

Think About the Solution: How does your character solve the problem? The solution can be something they learn or a clever idea they have.

Use Descriptive Words: Instead of saying 'big dog,' say 'huge, furry dog with bright eyes.' Descriptive words make your story more interesting.

Mix Up Your Sentences: Use short and long sentences. Start sentences in different ways to make your writing more exciting.

Read Out Loud: Sometimes, reading your story out loud can help you hear what works and what doesn't.

Take a Break: If you're stuck, take a short break. Do something fun, then come back to your story.

Ask "What If ": If you're stuck, ask 'What if?' about your story. What if the character made a different choice? What if the setting was different?

Draw a Picture: Sometimes, drawing a scene from your story can help you think of new ideas.

End with a Bang: Try to end your story in an exciting way or wrap everything up nicely.

Have Fun: Remember, writing is about being creative and having fun. There's no right or wrong way to tell your story.

Any Tips or Notes for Yourself? Write it here!

CHAPTER 3

How to Use This Book Example Prompt

"Mira's Magical Paintbrush Adventure"
Example Prompt

Prompt-

Mira, a young potion master, creates a brew that allows her to step into paintings and explore the worlds within. But when an evil sorcerer follows her into the paintings and begins stealing the art's magic, Mira must rally characters from famous paintings to stop him.

Story Setting Questions-

Describe Mira's surroundings. What kind of environment is she in? Is it busy or quiet, natural or artificial? What is the weather like?

Mira lives in a cozy cottage at the edge of Echoing Elm Woods. The environment is primarily natural, with a quiet, peaceful atmosphere. The weather is likely mild and pleasant, suitable for outdoor activities and exploration.

Write and Draw!

Is your story set in a specific historical period, the present day, or a future era? Be specific, especially if it is essential to the story.

> The story is set in a fantasy world that combines elements of magic with a timeless feel. It's not tied to a specific historical period or the present day but exists in its magical realm, where potions and enchanted paintings are part of everyday life.

What time of day is your story? Or is it multiple days? How does this impact the story?

> Most events in the story happen during the day. The daytime setting contributes to a bright, adventurous mood and allows for vivid descriptions of the colorful worlds within the paintings Mira explores.

Are there any significant landmarks or unique locations in your story? What makes them essential?

> The most significant locations in the story are the paintings themselves. Each painting is a portal to a new world, offering unique landscapes and adventures. Mira's cottage, where she practices potion-making, is also an important location as it's her home base and the starting point of her journey.

Does Mira find the setting to be a happy place, a scary one, or something in between? How does the setting make her feel?

Mira finds her setting to be a happy and exciting place overall. Her cottage and the surrounding woods make her feel comfortable and inspired. The magical paintings fill her with wonder and curiosity, but they also present challenges and moments of fear as she encounters new situations.

Setting Notes or Drawings...
The story's setting is rich with magical elements. Mira's cottage is likely filled with colorful potions, ingredients, and magical artifacts. The Echoing Elm Woods probably have their own mysterious and enchanting qualities. The paintings serve as portals to various fantastical settings, from meadows and oceans to mountains and gardens, each with its unique atmosphere and inhabitants.

Main Character Questions-
What words would you use to describe Mira's personality? Is she brave, curious, funny, shy, or something else?

Mira is super curious; she always wants to know what's in every nook and cranny! She's brilliant, always thinking up new potions. At first, she's very talented but unsure of herself. She doesn't see her immense talent and kind personality for all its worth.

What unique qualities or abilities does your main character have? What sets them apart from others in the story?

Mira can make magical potions! But her most remarkable trait is that she can jump into paintings like real places. Mira has olive skin and wavy brown hair. She is shorter than her peers and always wears her favorite lavender apron with pockets bulging with various potion ingredients. She has a vibrant personality, and her enthusiasm shines through in everything she does.

What does Mira love to do the most? Does she have a favorite place, hobby, or food?

Mira loves mixing potions. I bet her room is full of bubbling cauldrons and colorful liquids in weird-shaped bottles. Her favorite place is inside a fantastic painting of a meadow, where the grass tickles your feet and the air smells like flowers.

Where does Mira come from? Tell us about her family, where she grew up, or an important event from his past.

Mira lives beside a magical forest called Echoing Elm Woods in a cute little cottage. Can you imagine how cool that would be? I bet the trees whisper secrets to each other! Before she could jump into paintings, she would spend her days exploring the forest when she wasn't studying potions or playing with her friends.

What hopes or dreams does Mira have, and what is she most afraid of? Does this affect the story?

Mira loves to make potions but wishes she could be the best in the world! She also would like to be more brave. She's scared of messing up or not being good enough, which makes her nervous sometimes. But it also makes her try extra hard to help everyone, like when you want to win the spelling bee, so you practice every day. She is much better than she realizes; she lacks self-confidence.

Main Character Notes or Drawings...

Mira has this cool purple apron with pockets full of magic stuff! She is very talented at making potions, especially for her age. But she doesn't realize how good she is.

Side Character Questions-

Think about the other characters in your story besides the main character. Who are they, and what do they look like?

Zoran is a wizard that looks scary initially, with these intense purple eyes that look right through you. He wears this long, flowing silver cloak that shimmers when he moves like it's made of starlight. Pixel is this tiny fairy, no bigger than your hand, with wings that shine like a rainbow caught in a soap bubble. The owl is big and fluffy, with wise old eyes that make you feel like it knows everything in the entire world and beyond!

35

What are these other characters like? Are they funny, serious, kind, or maybe a little mischievous? Could you describe their personalities?

Zoran seems mean at first, like the villain in a movie, but then you find out he's friendly and is only stealing to help his home. Pixel is fun and mischievous, constantly zooming around and playing tricks, but she's also helpful when it matters. The owl is serious and intelligent, like that teacher who seems strict but gives the best advice.

What are the other characters' favorite activities, foods, or hobbies? How do these preferences show their personalities?

I bet Zoran secretly loves tending to magical plants in his world, nurturing them to keep the last bits of magic alive. Pixel probably loves playing hide-and-seek in the paintings, using her tiny size to squeeze into the tiniest hiding spots. The owl loves solving riddles and may even collect exciting facts from all the paintings he visits.

How does Mira interact with these other characters? Do they get along well, have disagreements, or help each other in tough situations?

Mira is initially scared of Zoran, as you might feel if you saw a ghost! But then she's brave enough to talk to him, and they become friends. Mira gets along well with all the other characters in the story. And they all help her save the day for Zoran's world!

How do the other side characters influence the story's events? Are they involved in the central conflict or help solve a big problem?

Zoran accidentally causes a big problem in the story, but he only tries to help his home. Zoran also creates tension at the story's beginning by being a mysterious character who is wreaking havoc in other paintings. Pixel and the owl are like Mira's sidekicks, helping her develop ideas and giving her courage when needed.

Side Character Notes or Drawings...

Zoran is the most important side character. He creates the initial story conflict. Mira responds to him taking magic from other paintings by being brave and confronting him. By confronting him, she becomes more brave.

Conflict and Resolution Questions-

What big problems and challenges does Mira face in the story?

The big problem is that Zoran is taking all the magic from the paintings, which is like sucking all the color out of a rainbow. The paintings are dull and lifeless. But if he were to stop stealing magic, his world would also go dull and lifeless.

How does Mira react to the central conflict? What are her emotions? What actions does she take?

When Mira first sees what Zoran's doing, she gets super scared, like when you wake up from a bad dream. Her heart probably beats fast, and she wants to run away. But she's also curious and worried about the paintings, so she decides to be brave and figure out what's happening.

How are the side characters involved in the central conflict? Do they help or make things more complicated for the main character?

Pixel and the owl are like Mira's team in a big game. Pixel flies around, checking on all the paintings and reporting back to Mira, while the owl uses his big brain to devise intelligent ideas.

What steps does Mira take to resolve the conflict? Does she need to make a tough decision or take a significant risk?

Mira takes several steps to resolve the conflict with Zoran. First, she bravely approaches him to understand why he's taking magic from the paintings. After learning about his world's problem, Mira suggests working together to find a solution. She then visits different paintings with Zoran, learning about their magic and asking for help from characters like Pixel the Fairy and the wise old owl. Finally, Mira takes a risk by creating a special potion using essence from various paintings, which, combined with Zoran's spell, creates the magical bridge to save both worlds.

Is there an unexpected twist or turn in how the conflict evolves or is resolved? What surprises the characters?

The big surprise is that Zoran isn't a bad guy at all! It's like in a mystery book when you find out the person you thought was the villain is trying to save everyone. Zoran is just trying to save his home, which is dying without magic.

How is the conflict finally resolved? What changes occur in the story because of this resolution?

They fix everything by making a magical rainbow bridge between paintings! Imagine a rainbow bridge, but instead of colors, it's made of sparkly magic that flows between all the worlds. The magical bridge between the worlds lets the paintings share the magic! The bridge also fixes all of the paintings Zoran had stolen from before.

How do the main and side characters feel about how the conflict was resolved? Are they relieved, happy, sad, or something else?

When they solve the problem, everyone is so happy! Mira is proud and self-confident for approaching Zoran and then creating the bridge. She is also excited to have made many new friends in the paintings. Her world is so much bigger now that she can jump into the paintings. Zoran is ecstatic to have saved his world, and the other characters are glad Zoran stopped stealing their magic.

What important lessons do the characters learn from facing and resolving the conflict? How do these lessons change them?

When Mira works with Zoran to solve the magic problem, she learns not to judge others too quickly and discovers the power of understanding and teamwork. Mira gains confidence in her abilities, tackling tougher challenges and even teaching others, while Zoran learns to consider how his actions affect others. Their adventure shows how facing difficulties together can lead to personal growth, new friendships, and positive changes for all.

How does the resolution of the conflict impact the characters and the world of your story in the long run?

Mira becomes more confident, continuing her adventures and teaching magic to others in Echoing Elm Woods. Zoran and Mira form a lasting friendship, working together to maintain the magical bridge and likely solving new challenges. The story's world becomes more interconnected and harmonious, with characters from different paintings cooperating and sharing magic.

How do the characters' relationships change after the conflict is resolved? Do they become closer, or are there new challenges they face?

Mira and Zoran become close friends, overcoming their initial mistrust. They continue to work together, maintaining the magical bridge and likely facing new adventures. Mira's relationships with the characters in the paintings grow stronger as she visits them more often. Her newfound confidence also affects her interactions with others in Echoing Elm Woods, where she starts teaching young magic users.

Conflict and Resolution Notes or Drawings...

The reader thinks the most significant conflict will be that Zoran is a scary, evil character. However, the actual conflict creates a bridge between the paintings.

Ending Questions-

Could you describe how your story ends? What happens in the final scenes?

Mira and Zoran activate the magical bridge they created, sharing magic between the paintings and Zoran's world. Colors flow between the worlds, bringing life back to Zoran's home and restoring the drained paintings. Zoran thanks Mira for her help and wisdom, and they promise to meet again to maintain the magical bridge. Mira returns to her cottage, feeling proud and confident about her accomplishment.

Could you describe the setting where the story ends? How is it different from the beginning?

The story ends in Mira's cozy cottage at the edge of Echoing Elm Woods, just like where it began. But now, the paintings in her cottage seem more alive than ever, each a window to new adventures. The cottage feels warmer and more magical, filled with the energy of Mira's recent adventure. Outside, the Echoing Elm Woods remain the same, but Mira sees them with new, more confident eyes.

How does Mira feel at the end of the story? Is she happy, sad, relieved, or something else?

At the end of the story, Mira feels happy, proud, and confident. She's relieved she solved the problem and helped Zoran save his world. Mira also feels excited about future adventures and the new magic she's learned.

How has Mira changed from the beginning of the story to the end?

Mira has become much more confident in herself and her abilities. She's no longer doubtful but sees herself as brave and capable of solving big problems. Mira has also learned to work with others and to look beyond first impressions. She's grown from a shy potion maker into a bold adventurer and even a teacher.

What happens to the side characters at the end of the story? How are their stories wrapped up?

Zoran returns to his world, which is now full of life and magic again. He and Mira promise to keep working together to maintain the magical bridge. The characters in the paintings, like Pixel the fairy and the wise old owl, continue their lives in their restored, vibrant worlds. They remain friends with Mira, who can visit them through the paintings.

Are any questions or mysteries left unanswered at the end of the story? Why were they left unresolved?

The story leaves open the possibility of future magical quests and adventures for Mira. We don't know exactly what these might be, which creates excitement and curiosity for potential sequels. The exact nature of Zoran's world and how it lost its magic isn't fully explained, leaving room for more exploration in future stories.

What is the main lesson or message of the story at its conclusion? What do you want your readers to take away?

The main message is that creativity, kindness, and teamwork can solve even the biggest problems. Readers should take away that it's important to look beyond first impressions, to be brave in facing challenges, and to work together with others. The story also shows that believing in yourself can help you do amazing things.

Ending Notes or Drawings...

Mira continues her potion-making with new enthusiasm, tackling more complex recipes. She starts teaching other young magic users in Echoing Elm Woods. Mira's adventures have just begun, and she looks forward to using her paintbrush to explore new magical worlds and help more people.

Story Notes

Use this section to write notes or drawings that wouldn't fit the other answer boxes. You can even write ideas for a sequel adventure for your story's characters!

It's time for you to write your own unique story! Before you start, could you outline how your story will go? It helps to outline your story in a beginning, middle, and end. Consider when you will introduce characters, where the story starts and ends, when you introduce your conflict and resolution, etc. Good luck; you are going to do great!

"Mira's Magical Paintbrush Adventure"
Outline all the major events in the story

HOW DOES YOUR STORY BEGIN?

MIRA, A YOUNG POTION MASTER WITH SELF-DOUBT, ACCIDENTALLY CREATES A MAGICAL PAINTBRUSH THAT ALLOWS HER TO JUMP INTO PAINTINGS. SHE EXPLORES VARIOUS PAINTED WORLDS, EXPERIENCING EXCITING ADVENTURES IN EACH ONE. HOWEVER, MIRA SOON NOTICES A SINISTER SHADOW FOLLOWING HER FROM PAINTING TO PAINTING.

THE SHADOW BELONGS TO ZORAN, A SORCERER ABSORBING MAGIC FROM THE PAINTINGS TO SAVE HIS DYING WORLD. UNDERSTANDING ZORAN'S MOTIVE FOR SAVING HIS HOME, MIRA DECIDES TO HELP HIM FIND A SOLUTION THAT DOESN'T HARM OTHER WORLDS. TOGETHER WITH MAGICAL BEINGS FROM DIFFERENT PAINTINGS, THEY DISCOVER THAT MAGIC CAN BE SHARED WITHOUT DEPLETING ITS SOURCE.

HOW DOES YOUR STORY END?

WHAT HAPPENS IN THE MIDDLE?

MIRA CREATES A SPECIAL POTION THAT, COMBINED WITH ZORAN'S SPELL, ESTABLISHES A MAGICAL BRIDGE BETWEEN THE PAINTINGS AND ZORAN'S WORLD. THIS SOLUTION REVITALIZES ZORAN'S WORLD WHILE PRESERVING THE MAGIC IN THE PAINTINGS, DEMONSTRATING THE POWER OF COOPERATION AND CREATIVITY. THE ADVENTURE BOOSTS MIRA'S CONFIDENCE, LEADING HER TO BECOME MORE ADVENTUROUS IN HER POTION-MAKING AND EVEN BEGIN TEACHING OTHERS, ALL WHILE MAINTAINING THE MAGICAL BRIDGE WITH ZORAN.

45A

"Mira's Magical Paintbrush Adventure"

Have you ever wondered what it would be like to jump into a painting? To feel the brush strokes beneath your feet and smell the colors in the air? That's precisely what happened to Mira, the young potion master with a heart full of curiosity and a head full of dreams.

Mira was a bright-eyed girl with warm olive skin and long, wavy chestnut hair. She was on the shorter side and full of boundless energy and enthusiasm, her vibrant personality shining through in everything she did. She always wore her favorite lavender apron, its pockets bulging with various potion ingredients, and her trusted notebook.

She lived in a cozy cottage at the edge of Echoing Elm Woods, where she spent her days mixing potions and practicing magic. Mira was clever and creative but often doubted herself despite her immense talent, wishing she could be as brave and confident as the heroes in her favorite paintings.

One day, while experimenting with a new potion, Mira accidentally spilled some onto her favorite paintbrush. To her amazement, the bristles began to glow with a soft, golden light. Hesitantly, she touched the brush to a painting of a sun-dappled meadow hanging on her wall. In a flash of light, Mira found herself standing in that very meadow, surrounded by waving grass and colorful wildflowers!

Excited by her discovery, Mira began exploring other paintings. She danced with dolphins in an ocean scene and climbed snow-capped mountains in a landscape. To move between paintings, Mira simply touched her glowing brush to the edge of one artwork, and with a swirl of color, she'd find herself stepping into the next. But her adventures took a dark turn when she noticed a sinister shadow following her from painting to painting.

The shadow belonged to Zoran, a sorcerer with piercing violet eyes, a sharp, angular face, and a flowing silver cloak that shimmered brightly. His long, silver hair was tied back in a neat ponytail, adding to his air of mystique and power. Zoran had discovered Mira's secret and was using it to absorb the magic from the paintings, leaving them dull and lifeless.

At first, Mira thought Zoran was simply evil. But as she watched him more closely, she noticed the sadness in his eyes and the gentleness with which he touched the fading paintings.

Gathering her courage, Mira approached Zoran in a painting of a tranquil garden. "Why are you taking the magic?" she asked, her voice trembling slightly.

Zoran sighed, his shoulders sagging. "My world is dying," he explained. "The magic is fading and taking all the beauty and life from my world." I thought if I could gather enough magic from these paintings, I could restore my home."

Mira's heart softened. She understood the desire to protect one's home. "But taking the magic hurts these worlds, too," she said gently. "There must be another way."

Zoran looked at her with hope. "Do you think you could help? You're a potion master, after all."

Mira bit her lip, thinking hard. She wasn't sure if she could, but she knew she had to try. "Let's work together," she suggested. We can find a way to share the magic without harming anyone.

Over the next few days, Mira and Zoran visited different paintings and learned about their magic. They also met with Pixel, the fairy whose tiny wings shimmered like rainbows, a wise old owl, and other characters, explaining the situation and asking for help.

They had a breakthrough in a painting of a brilliant sunrise. The wise owl hooted, "Magic isn't a finite resource. It's like the sun—it can shine on many worlds without dimming."

Excited by this idea, Mira mixed a special potion using essence from various paintings. When combined with Zoran's spell, it created a magical bridge between the paintings and Zoran's world.

As they activated the bridge, colors flowed between the worlds. The paintings remained vibrant, while Zoran's world began to sparkle with new life. Even the paintings that Zoran had initially drained began to regain their vibrancy, the colors seeping back into them like water into parched earth. Zoran's face lit up with joy and relief.

"Thank you, Mira," he said, his violet eyes shining with gratitude. "You've saved my world without sacrificing others. I misjudged you initially - you're wiser than I ever could have imagined."

Mira beamed, feeling a warm glow of pride and confidence. She had faced her fears, solved a complex problem, and made a new friend. As she and Zoran said goodbye, promising to meet again to maintain the magical bridge, Mira realized how much she had grown.

From that day on, Mira continued her adventures with renewed enthusiasm. She visited her painting friends, worked on new potions, and occasionally met with Zoran to check on their magical bridge. Her newfound confidence spilled over into her potion-making. She tackled more complex recipes, experimented boldly with new ingredients, and even started teaching other young magic users in Echoing Elm Woods.

Every time she looked at a painting, she remembered the magic on the canvas and the magic of kindness, creativity, and cooperation that lived inside herself. The paintings in her cottage seemed more alive than ever, each one a window to new adventures and learning opportunities.

Mira stood taller now, smiled brighter, and felt a warm glow of confidence in her heart. She had proven to herself that she was just as brave and heroic as any painting character. And she knew that with imagination, compassion, and teamwork, she could overcome any challenge that came her way.

As she mixed her latest potion, her lavender apron now adorned with colorful splatters from her many adventures, Mira couldn't help but wonder what magical quest awaited her next. With her trusty paintbrush in one hand and a bubbling potion in the other, she knew she was ready for anything.

CHAPTER 4

Merrick's Invisible Village Mayhem

"Merrick's Invisible Village Mayhem"

Prompt-

Merrick, a clumsy young wizard, accidentally turns his entire village invisible while attempting to cure his cat's hiccups. As panicked voices fill the air and floating objects zip around, Merrick realizes he's the only one who can still see the village and its inhabitants. With his spellbook missing and his mentor away, Merrick must find a way to reverse the spell before sunset, when the invisibility becomes permanent.

Story Setting Questions-

Describe Merrick's surroundings. What kind of environment is he in? Is it busy or quiet, natural or artificial? What is the weather like?

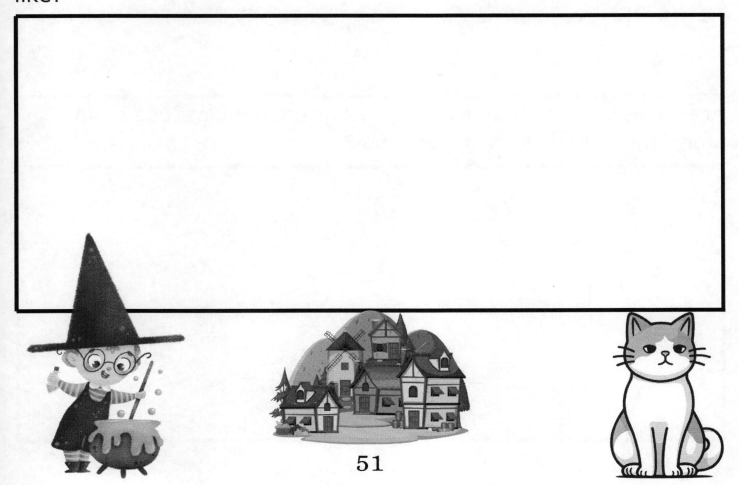

Is your story set in a specific historical period, the present day, or a future era? Be specific, especially if it is essential to the story.

What time of day is your story? Or is it multiple days? How does this impact the story?

Are there any significant landmarks or unique locations in your story? What makes them essential?

Does Merrick find the setting to be a happy place, a scary one, or something in between? How does the setting make him feel?

Setting Notes or Drawings...

Main Character Questions-

What words would you use to describe Merrick's personality? Is he brave, curious, funny, shy, or something else?

What unique qualities or abilities does your main character have? What sets them apart from others in the story?

What does Merrick love to do the most? Does he have a favorite place, hobby, or food?

Where does Merrick come from? Tell us about his family, where he grew up, or an important event from his past.

What hopes or dreams does Merrick have, and what is he most afraid of? Does this affect the story?

Main Character Notes or Drawings...

Side Character Questions-

Think about the other characters in your story besides the main character. Who are they, and what do they look like?

What are these other characters like? Are they funny, serious, kind, or maybe a little mischievous? Could you describe their personalities?

What are the other characters' favorite activities, foods, or hobbies? How do these preferences show their personalities?

How does Merrick interact with these other characters? Do they get along, have disagreements, or help each other in challenging situations?

How do the other side characters influence the story's events? Are they involved in the central conflict or help solve a big problem?

Side Character Notes or Drawings...

Conflict and Resolution Questions-

What big problems and challenges does Merrick face in the story?

How does Merrick react when he first encounters the central conflict? What emotions or actions does he show?

How are the side characters involved in the central conflict? Do they help or make things more complicated for the main character?

What steps does Merrick take to resolve the conflict? Does he need to make a tough decision or take a significant risk?

Is there an unexpected twist or turn in how the conflict evolves or is resolved? What surprises the characters?

How is the conflict finally resolved? What changes occur in the story because of this resolution?

How do the main and side characters feel about how the conflict was resolved? Are they relieved, happy, sad, or something else?

What important lessons do the characters learn from facing and resolving the conflict? How do these lessons change them?

How does the resolution of the conflict impact the characters and the world of your story in the long run?

How do the characters' relationships change after the conflict is resolved? Do they become closer, or are there new challenges they face?

Conflict and Resolution Notes or Drawings...

Ending Questions-

Could you describe how your story ends? What happens in the final scenes?

Could you describe the setting where the story ends? How is it different from the beginning?

How does Merrick feel at the end of the story? Is he happy, sad, relieved, or something else?

How has Merrick changed from the beginning of the story to the end?

What happens to the side characters at the end of the story? How are their stories wrapped up?

Are any questions or mysteries left unanswered at the end of the story? Why were they left unresolved?

What is the main lesson or message of the story at its conclusion? What do you want your readers to take away?

Ending Notes or Drawings...

Story Notes

It's time for you to write your own unique story! Before you start, could you outline how your story will go? It helps to outline your story in a beginning, middle, and end. Consider when you will introduce characters, where the story starts and ends, when you introduce your conflict and resolution, etc. Good luck; you are going to do great!

"Merrick's Invisible Village Mayhem"

Outline all the major events in the story

HOW DOES YOUR STORY BEGIN?

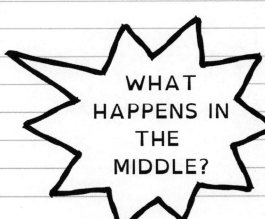

WHAT HAPPENS IN THE MIDDLE?

HOW DOES YOUR STORY END?

"Merrick's Invisible Village Mayhem"

"YOU CAN MAKE ANYTHING
BY WRITING."
- C.S. LEWIS

"THE MORE YOU READ,
THE MORE THINGS YOU
WILL KNOW. THE MORE
THAT YOU LEARN, THE
MORE PLACES YOU'LL
GO- DR. SEUSS

"Merrick's Invisible Village Mayhem"

"BELIEVE YOU CAN
AND YOU'RE
HALFWAY THERE."

- THEODORE
ROOSEVELT

"THE BEST WAY TO
PREDICT YOUR FUTURE
IS TO CREATE IT."

- ABRAHAM LINCOLN

"Merrick's Invisible Village Mayhem"

"EVERY DAY MAY NOT BE GOOD, BUT THERE'S SOMETHING GOOD IN EVERY DAY."
- ALICE MORSE EARLE

"YOUR IMAGINATION IS YOUR PREVIEW OF LIFE'S COMING ATTRACTIONS."
- ALBERT EINSTEIN

"Merrick's Invisible Village Mayhem"

"THE ONLY WAY TO DO GREAT WORK IS TO LOVE WHAT YOU DO."
- STEVE JOBS

IF YOU ENJOYED THIS FANTASY PROMPT, YOU WILL LOVE THIS BOOK WITH 6 UNIQUE FANTASY PROMPTS

NEED MORE SPACE TO WRITE? GRAB AN EMPTY NOTEBOOK OR CHECK OUT THIS KEEPSAKE JOURNAL!

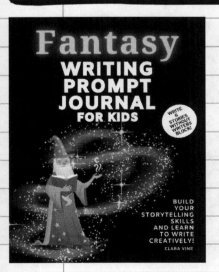

UNLOCK YOUR PHONE AND USE THE CAMERA FOR LINK!

70

CHAPTER 5

Zara and the Runaway Shadow Adventure

"Zara and the Runaway Shadow Adventure"

Prompt-

When Zara's shadow detaches and runs away, she chases it through a magical city where everyone's shadows live secret lives. She must reunite with her shadow before the next full moon or remain incomplete forever. Can she do it?

Story Setting Questions-

Describe Zara's surroundings. What kind of environment is she in? Is it busy or quiet, natural or artificial? What is the weather like?

Is your story set in a specific historical period, the present day, or a future era? Be specific, especially if it is essential to the story.

What time of day is your story? Or is it multiple days? How does this impact the story?

Are there any significant landmarks or unique locations in your story? What makes them essential?

Does Zara find the setting to be a happy place, a scary one, or something in between? How does the setting make her feel?

```


```

Setting Notes or Drawings...

Main Character Questions-

What words would you use to describe Zara's personality? Is she brave, curious, funny, shy, or something else?

```


```

What unique qualities or abilities does your main character have? What sets them apart from others in the story?

What does Zara love to do the most? Does she have a favorite place, hobby, or food?

Where does Zara come from? Tell us about her family, where she grew up, or an important event from her past.

What hopes or dreams does Zara have, and what is she most afraid of? Does this affect the story?

Main Character Notes or Drawings...

Side Character Questions-

Think about the other characters in your story besides the main character. Who are they, and what do they look like?

What are these other characters like? Are they funny, serious, kind, or maybe a little mischievous? Could you describe their personalities?

What are the other characters' favorite activities, foods, or hobbies? How do these preferences show their personalities?

How does Zara interact with these other characters? Do they get along, have disagreements, or help each other in challenging situations?

How do the other side characters influence the story's events? Are they involved in the central conflict or help solve a big problem?

Side Character Notes or Drawings...

Conflict and Resolution Questions-

What big problems and challenges does Zara face in the story?

How does Zara react when she first encounters the central conflict? What emotions or actions does she show?

How are the side characters involved in the central conflict? Do they help or make things more complicated for the main character?

What steps does Zara take to resolve the conflict? Does she need to make a tough decision or take a significant risk?

Is there an unexpected twist or turn in how the conflict evolves or is resolved? What surprises the characters?

How is the conflict finally resolved? What changes occur in the story because of this resolution?

How do the main and side characters feel about how the conflict was resolved? Are they relieved, happy, sad, or something else?

What important lessons do the characters learn from facing and resolving the conflict? How do these lessons change them?

How does the resolution of the conflict impact the characters and the world of your story in the long run?

How do the characters' relationships change after the conflict is resolved? Do they become closer, or are there new challenges they face?

Conflict and Resolution Notes or Drawings...

Ending Questions-

Could you describe how your story ends? What happens in the final scenes?

Could you describe the setting where the story ends? How is it different from the beginning?

How does Zara feel at the end of the story? Is she happy, sad, relieved, or something else?

How has Zara changed from the beginning of the story to the end?

What happens to the side characters at the end of the story? How are their stories wrapped up?

Are any questions or mysteries left unanswered at the end of the story? Why were they left unresolved?

What is the main lesson or message of the story at its conclusion? What do you want your readers to take away?

Ending Notes or Drawings...

Story Notes

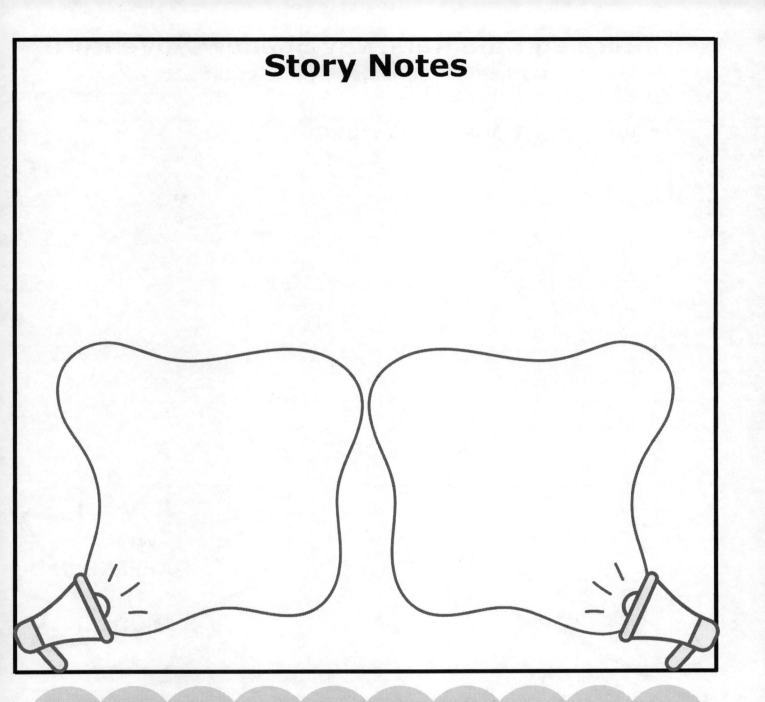

It's time for you to write your own unique story! Before you start, could you outline how your story will go? It helps to outline your story in a beginning, middle, and end. Consider when you will introduce characters, where the story starts and ends, when you introduce your conflict and resolution, etc. Good luck; you are going to do great!

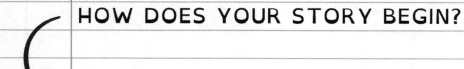

"Zara and the Runaway Shadow Adventure"
Outline all the major events in the story

HOW DOES YOUR STORY BEGIN?

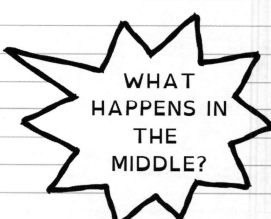

WHAT HAPPENS IN THE MIDDLE?

HOW DOES YOUR STORY END?

"

"TODAY A READER, TOMORROW A LEADER."
- MARGARET FULLER

"

"DON'T LET WHAT YOU CAN'T DO STOP YOU FROM DOING WHAT YOU CAN DO."

- JOHN WOODEN

"Zara and the Runaway Shadow Adventure"

"THE EXPERT IN ANYTHING WAS ONCE A BEGINNER."

- HELEN HAYES

"YOU'RE OFF TO GREAT PLACES! TODAY IS YOUR DAY! YOUR MOUNTAIN IS WAITING, SO GET ON YOUR WAY!"

- DR. SEUSS

"Zara and the Runaway Shadow Adventure"

THE MORE DIFFICULT THE
VICTORY, THE GREATER THE
HAPPINESS IN WINNING."
- PELE

"YOU MUST DO THE
THINGS YOU THINK YOU
CANNOT DO."
- ELEANOR ROOSEVELT

"Zara and the Runaway Shadow Adventure"

"THE ONLY WAY TO DO GREAT WORK IS TO LOVE WHAT YOU DO."
- STEVE JOBS

IF YOU ENJOYED THIS FANTASY PROMPT, YOU WILL LOVE THIS BOOK WITH 6 UNIQUE FANTASY PROMPTS

NEED MORE SPACE TO WRITE? GRAB AN EMPTY NOTEBOOK OR CHECK OUT THIS KEEPSAKE JOURNAL!

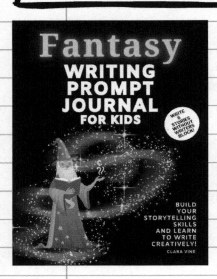

UNLOCK YOUR PHONE AND USE THE CAMERA FOR LINK!

91

CHAPTER 6

Alfie and the Secret Language

"Alfie and the Secret Language"

Prompt-

Alfie, a scruffy but lovable dog, discovers he can understand and speak to all the neighborhood pets after drinking from a mysterious glowing puddle. At first, he's thrilled to chat with his furry and feathered friends, but then he overhears a group of mischievous cats plotting to take over the local park. With his new ability, Alfie must rally a team of unlikely animal allies—including a timid hamster, a grumpy old parrot, and a hyperactive squirrel—to outsmart the cats and save the park. But can Alfie keep his extraordinary power a secret from his human family while leading this ragtag group of critters on their critical mission?

Story Setting Questions-

Describe Alfie's surroundings. What kind of environment is he in? Is it busy or quiet, natural or artificial? What is the weather like?

Is your story set in a specific historical period, the present day, or a future era? Be specific, especially if it is essential to the story.

What time of day is your story? Or is it multiple days? How does this impact the story?

Are there any significant landmarks or unique locations in your story? What makes them essential?

Does Alfie find the setting to be a happy place, a scary one, or something in between? How does the setting make him feel?

Setting Notes or Drawings...

Main Character Questions-

What words would you use to describe Alfie's personality? Is he brave, curious, funny, shy, or something else?

What unique qualities or abilities does your main character have? What sets them apart from others in the story?

What does Alfie love to do the most? Does he have a favorite place, hobby, or food?

Where does Alfie come from? Tell us about his family, where he grew up, or an important event from his past.

What hopes or dreams does Alfie have, and what is he most afraid of? Does this affect the story?

Main Character Notes or Drawings...

Side Character Questions-

Think about the other characters in your story besides the main character. Who are they, and what do they look like?

97

What are these other characters like? Are they funny, serious, kind, or maybe a little mischievous? Could you describe their personalities?

What are the other characters' favorite activities, foods, or hobbies? How do these preferences show their personalities?

How does Alfie interact with these other characters? Do they get along, have disagreements, or help each other in challenging situations?

How do the other side characters influence the story's events? Are they involved in the central conflict or help solve a big problem?

Side Character Notes or Drawings...

Conflict and Resolution Questions-

What big problems and challenges does Alfie face in the story?

How does Alfie react when he first encounters the central conflict? What emotions or actions does he show?

How are the side characters involved in the central conflict? Do they help or make things more complicated for the main character?

What steps does Alfie take to resolve the conflict? Does he need to make a tough decision or take a significant risk?

Is there an unexpected twist or turn in how the conflict evolves or is resolved? What surprises the characters?

How is the conflict finally resolved? What changes occur in the story because of this resolution?

How do the main and side characters feel about how the conflict was resolved? Are they relieved, happy, sad, or something else?

What important lessons do the characters learn from facing and resolving the conflict? How do these lessons change them?

How does the resolution of the conflict impact the characters and the world of your story in the long run?

How do the characters' relationships change after the conflict is resolved? Do they become closer, or are there new challenges they face?

Conflict and Resolution Notes or Drawings...

Ending Questions-

Could you describe how your story ends? What happens in the final scenes?

Could you describe the setting where the story ends? How is it different from the beginning?

How does Alfie feel at the end of the story? Is he happy, sad, relieved, or something else?

How has Alfie changed from the beginning of the story to the end?

What happens to the side characters at the end of the story? How are their stories wrapped up?

Are any questions or mysteries left unanswered at the end of the story? Why were they left unresolved?

What is the main lesson or message of the story at its conclusion? What do you want your readers to take away?

Ending Notes or Drawings...

Story Notes

It's time for you to write your own unique story! Before you start, could you outline how your story will go? It helps to outline your story in a beginning, middle, and end. Consider when you will introduce characters, where the story starts and ends, when you introduce your conflict and resolution, etc. Good luck; you are going to do great!

"Alfie and the Secret Language"

Outline all the major events in the story

HOW DOES YOUR STORY BEGIN?

WHAT HAPPENS IN THE MIDDLE?

HOW DOES YOUR STORY END?

"Alfie and the Secret Language"

"Alfie and the Secret Language"

"THE GREATEST
ADVENTURE YOU
CAN TAKE IS TO
LIVE THE LIFE OF
YOUR DREAMS."

- OPRAH WINFREY

"YOU ARE NEVER
TOO OLD TO SET
ANOTHER GOAL OR
TO DREAM A NEW
DREAM."

- C.S. LEWIS

"Alfie and the Secret Language"

"DON'T WATCH THE CLOCK;
DO WHAT IT DOES. KEEP
GOING."

- SAM LEVENSON

"THE DIFFERENCE BETWEEN
ORDINARY AND
EXTRAORDINARY IS THAT
LITTLE EXTRA."
JIMMY JOHNSON

"Alfie and the Secret Language"

"YOU ARE BRAVER THAN YOU BELIEVE, STRONGER THAN YOU SEEM, AND SMARTER THAN YOU THINK."
- A.A. MILNE (WINNIE THE POOH)

IF YOU ENJOYED THIS ANIMAL PROMPT, YOU WILL LOVE THIS BOOK WITH 6 UNIQUE ANIMAL PROMPTS

NEED MORE SPACE TO WRITE? GRAB AN EMPTY NOTEBOOK OR CHECK OUT THIS KEEPSAKE JOURNAL!

UNLOCK YOUR PHONE AND USE THE CAMERA FOR LINK!

CHAPTER 7

Echo's Time-Echoing Bat Mission

"Echo's Time-Echoing Bat Mission"

Prompt-

Echo, the bat, discovers she can echolocate through time, catching glimpses of the past and future. When she foresees a disaster threatening the cave ecosystem, Echo must convince the other animals to believe her warnings and work together to change the future.

Story Setting Questions-

Describe Echo's surroundings. What kind of environment is she in? Is it busy or quiet, natural or artificial? What is the weather like?

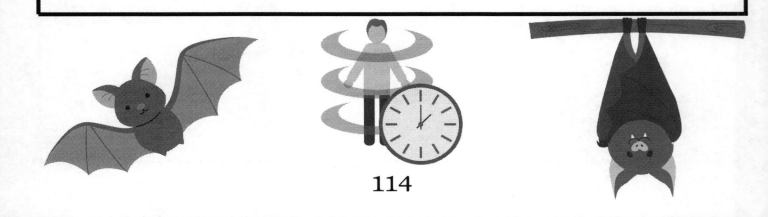

114

Is your story set in a specific historical period, the present day, or a future era? Be specific, especially if it is essential to the story.

What time of day is your story? Or is it multiple days? How does this impact the story?

Are there any significant landmarks or unique locations in your story? What makes them essential?

Does Echo find the setting to be a happy place, a scary one, or something in between? How does the setting make her feel?

Setting Notes or Drawings...

Main Character Questions-

What words would you use to describe Echo's personality? Is she brave, curious, funny, shy, or something else?

What unique qualities or abilities does your main character have? What sets them apart from others in the story?

What does Echo love to do the most? Does she have a favorite place, hobby, or food?

Where does Echo come from? Tell us about her family, where she grew up, or an important event from her past.

What hopes or dreams does Echo have, and what is she most afraid of? Does this affect the story?

Main Character Notes or Drawings...

Side Character Questions-

Think about the other characters in your story besides the main character. Who are they, and what do they look like?

What are these other characters like? Are they funny, serious, kind, or maybe a little mischievous? Could you describe their personalities?

What are the other characters' favorite activities, foods, or hobbies? How do these preferences show their personalities?

How does Echo interact with these other characters? Do they get along, have disagreements, or help each other in challenging situations?

How do the other side characters influence the story's events? Are they involved in the central conflict or help solve a big problem?

Side Character Notes or Drawings...

Conflict and Resolution Questions-

What big problems and challenges does Echo face in the story?

How does Echo react when she first encounters the central conflict? What emotions or actions does she show?

How are the side characters involved in the central conflict? Do they help or make things more complicated for the main character?

What steps does Echo take to resolve the conflict? Does she need to make a tough decision or take a significant risk?

Is there an unexpected twist or turn in how the conflict evolves or is resolved? What surprises the characters?

How is the conflict finally resolved? What changes occur in the story because of this resolution?

How do the main and side characters feel about how the conflict was resolved? Are they relieved, happy, sad, or something else?

What important lessons do the characters learn from facing and resolving the conflict? How do these lessons change them?

How does the resolution of the conflict impact the characters and the world of your story in the long run?

How do the characters' relationships change after the conflict is resolved? Do they become closer, or are there new challenges they face?

Conflict and Resolution Notes or Drawings...

Ending Questions-

Could you describe how your story ends? What happens in the final scenes?

Could you describe the setting where the story ends? How is it different from the beginning?

How does Echo feel at the end of the story? Is she happy, sad, relieved, or something else?

How has Echo changed from the beginning of the story to the end?

What happens to the side characters at the end of the story? How are their stories wrapped up?

Are any questions or mysteries left unanswered at the end of the story? Why were they left unresolved?

What is the main lesson or message of the story at its conclusion? What do you want your readers to take away?

Ending Notes or Drawings...

Story Notes

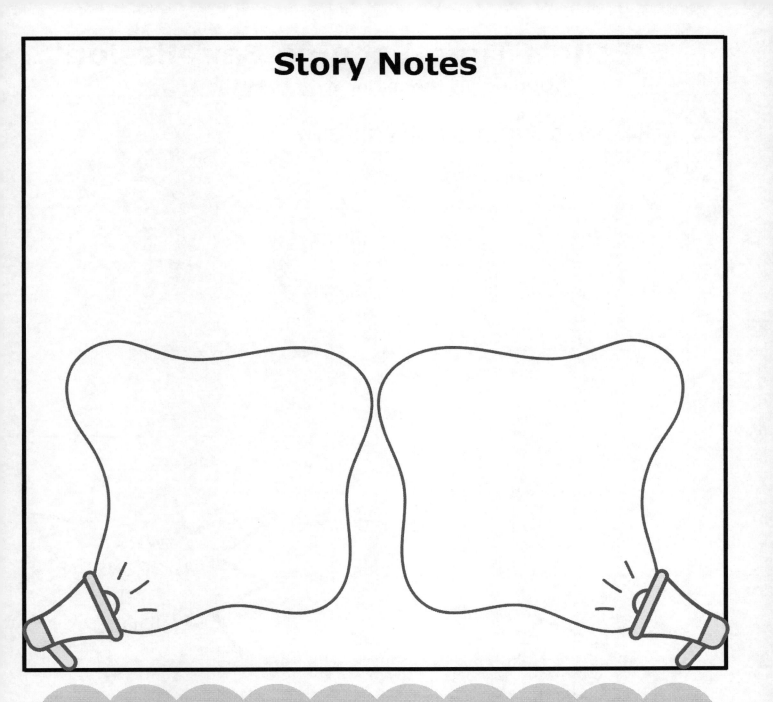

It's time for you to write your own unique story! Before you start, could you outline how your story will go? It helps to outline your story in a beginning, middle, and end. Consider when you will introduce characters, where the story starts and ends, when you introduce your conflict and resolution, etc. Good luck; you are going to do great!

"Echo's Time-Echoing Bat Mission"

Outline all the major events in the story

HOW DOES YOUR STORY BEGIN?

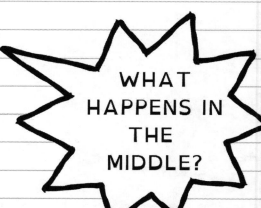

WHAT HAPPENS IN THE MIDDLE?

HOW DOES YOUR STORY END?

"Echo's Time-Echoing Bat Mission"

"NO ONE IS PERFECT - THAT'S WHY
PENCILS HAVE ERASERS."

- WOLFGANG RIEBE

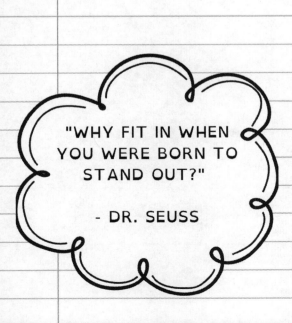

"WHY FIT IN WHEN
YOU WERE BORN TO
STAND OUT?"

- DR. SEUSS

"Echo's Time-Echoing Bat Mission"

"THE MOST CERTAIN WAY TO SUCCEED IS ALWAYS TO TRY JUST ONE MORE TIME."

- THOMAS A. EDISON

"IT ALWAYS SEEMS IMPOSSIBLE UNTIL IT'S DONE."

- NELSON MANDELA

"Echo's Time-Echoing Bat Mission"

"IMAGINATION IS EVERYTHING.
IT IS THE PREVIEW OF LIFE'S
COMING ATTRACTIONS."
- ALBERT EINSTEIN

"THE MORE YOU PRAISE AND
CELEBRATE YOUR LIFE, THE
MORE THERE IS IN LIFE TO
CELEBRATE."
- OPRAH WINFREY

"Echo's Time-Echoing Bat Mission"

"YOU MUST BE THE CHANGE YOU WISH TO SEE IN THE WORLD."

- MAHATMA GANDHI

IF YOU ENJOYED THIS ANIMAL PROMPT, YOU WILL LOVE THIS BOOK WITH 6 UNIQUE ANIMAL PROMPTS

NEED MORE SPACE TO WRITE? GRAB AN EMPTY NOTEBOOK OR CHECK OUT THIS KEEPSAKE JOURNAL!

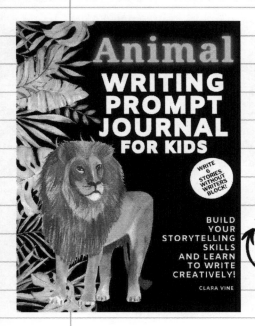

UNLOCK YOUR PHONE AND USE THE CAMERA FOR LINK!

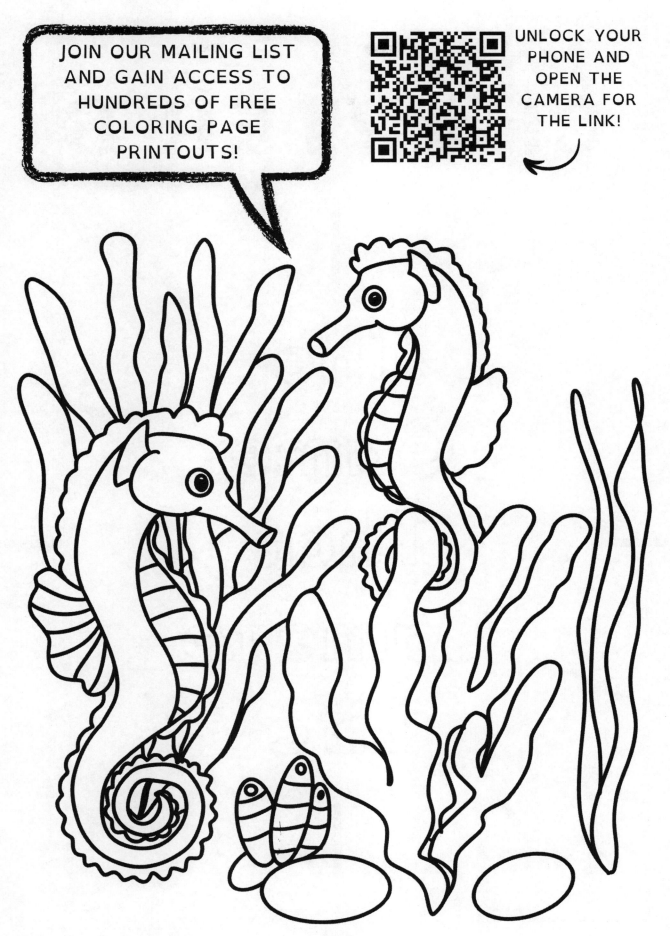

CHAPTER 8

The Game That Came to Life

"The Game That Came to Life"

Prompt-

Owen receives a mysterious handheld game console for his 10th birthday. When he starts playing, he discovers that creatures from the game are appearing in the real world! At first, it's fun to see cute pixel animals in the backyard, but things get out of hand when game villains start causing trouble in town. Owen and his best friend must figure out how to beat all the game's levels to send everything back where it belongs before their parents find out and the whole town turns into one big video game!

Story Setting Questions-

Describe Owens's surroundings. What kind of environment is he in? Is it busy or quiet, natural or artificial? What is the weather like?

Is your story set in a specific historical period, the present day, or a future era? Be specific, especially if it is essential to the story.

What time of day is your story? Or is it multiple days? How does this impact the story?

Are there any significant landmarks or unique locations in your story? What makes them essential?

Does Owen find the setting to be a happy place, a scary one, or something in between? How does the setting make him feel?

Setting Notes or Drawings...

Main Character Questions-

What words would you use to describe Owen's personality? Is he brave, curious, funny, shy, or something else?

What unique qualities or abilities does your main character have? What sets them apart from others in the story?

What does Owen love to do the most? Does he have a favorite place, hobby, or food?

Where does Owen come from? Tell us about his family, where he grew up, or an important event from his past.

What hopes or dreams does Owen have, and what is he most afraid of? Does this affect the story?

```


```

Main Character Notes or Drawings...

```


```

Side Character Questions-

Think about the other characters in your story besides the main character. Who are they, and what do they look like?

```


```

What are these other characters like? Are they funny, serious, kind, or maybe a little mischievous? Could you describe their personalities?

What are the other characters' favorite activities, foods, or hobbies? How do these preferences show their personalities?

How does Owen interact with these other characters? Do they get along, have disagreements, or help each other in challenging situations?

How do the other side characters influence the story's events? Are they involved in the central conflict or help solve a big problem?

Side Character Notes or Drawings...

Conflict and Resolution Questions-

What big problems and challenges does Owen face in the story?

How does Owen react when he first encounters the central conflict? What emotions or actions does he show?

How are the side characters involved in the central conflict? Do they help or make things more complicated for the main character?

What steps does Owen take to resolve the conflict? Does he need to make a tough decision or take a significant risk?

Is there an unexpected twist or turn in how the conflict evolves or is resolved? What surprises the characters?

How is the conflict finally resolved? What changes occur in the story because of this resolution?

How do the main and side characters feel about how the conflict was resolved? Are they relieved, happy, sad, or something else?

What important lessons do the characters learn from facing and resolving the conflict? How do these lessons change them?

How does the resolution of the conflict impact the characters and the world of your story in the long run?

How do the characters' relationships change after the conflict is resolved? Do they become closer, or are there new challenges they face?

Conflict and Resolution Notes or Drawings...

Ending Questions-

Could you describe how your story ends? What happens in the final scenes?

Could you describe the setting where the story ends? How is it different from the beginning?

How does Owen feel at the end of the story? Is he happy, sad, relieved, or something else?

How has Owen changed from the beginning of the story to the end?

What happens to the side characters at the end of the story? How are their stories wrapped up?

Are any questions or mysteries left unanswered at the end of the story? Why were they left unresolved?

What is the main lesson or message of the story at its conclusion? What do you want your readers to take away?

Ending Notes or Drawings...

Story Notes

It's time for you to write your own unique story! Before you start, could you outline how your story will go? It helps to outline your story in a beginning, middle, and end. Consider when you will introduce characters, where the story starts and ends, when you introduce your conflict and resolution, etc. Good luck; you are going to do great!

"The Game That Came to Life"
Outline all the major events in the story

HOW DOES YOUR STORY BEGIN?

WHAT HAPPENS IN THE MIDDLE?

HOW DOES YOUR STORY END?

"The Game That Came to Life"

"IT'S NOT WHAT HAPPENS TO YOU,
BUT HOW YOU REACT TO IT THAT
MATTERS."
- EPICTETUS

"THE FUTURE BELONGS
TO THOSE WHO
BELIEVE IN THE BEAUTY
OF THEIR DREAMS."

- ELEANOR ROOSEVELT

"The Game That Came to Life"

"REMEMBER THAT
HAPPINESS IS A
WAY OF TRAVEL,
NOT A
DESTINATION."

- ROY M. GOODMAN

"THERE IS ALWAYS
LIGHT. IF ONLY WE'RE
BRAVE ENOUGH TO SEE
IT. IF ONLY WE'RE
BRAVE ENOUGH TO BE
IT."

-AMANDA GORMAN

"The Game That Came to Life"

"THE BEST WAY TO CHEER YOURSELF UP IS TO TRY TO CHEER SOMEBODY ELSE UP."
- MARK TWAIN

"IT'S NOT WHETHER YOU GET KNOCKED DOWN, IT'S WHETHER YOU GET UP."
- VINCE LOMBARDI

"The Game That Came to Life"

"THE MORE YOU GIVE AWAY,
THE MORE YOU WILL HAVE."
- WILSON MIZNER

IF YOU ENJOYED THIS SCIENCE FICTION PROMPT, YOU WILL LOVE THIS BOOK WITH 6 UNIQUE SCIFI PROMPTS

NEED MORE SPACE TO WRITE? GRAB AN EMPTY NOTEBOOK OR CHECK OUT THIS KEEPSAKE JOURNAL!

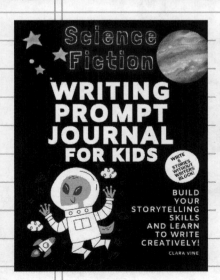

UNLOCK YOUR PHONE AND USE THE CAMERA FOR LINK!

154

CHAPTER 9

Zoe's Time-Pausing Smartwatch Scramble

"Zoe's Time-Pausing Smartwatch Scramble"

Prompt-

Zoe's new smartwatch accidentally connects to an alien satellite, and suddenly, she can pause time. She must learn to control this power before attracting unwanted attention from Earth and beyond.

Story Setting Questions-

Describe Zoe's surroundings. What kind of environment is she in? Is it busy or quiet, natural or artificial? What is the weather like?

Is your story set in a specific historical period, the present day, or a future era? Be specific, especially if it is essential to the story.

What time of day is your story? Or is it multiple days? How does this impact the story?

Are there any significant landmarks or unique locations in your story? What makes them essential?

Does Zoe find the setting to be a happy place, a scary one, or something in between? How does the setting make her feel?

Setting Notes or Drawings...

Main Character Questions-

What words would you use to describe Zoe's personality? Is she brave, curious, funny, shy, or something else?

What unique qualities or abilities does your main character have? What sets them apart from others in the story?

Where does Zoe love to do the most? Does she have a favorite place, hobby, or food?

Where does Zoe come from? Tell us about her family, where she grew up, or an important event from her past.

What hopes or dreams does Zoe have, and what is she most afraid of? Does this affect the story?

Main Character Notes or Drawings...

Side Character Questions-

Think about the other characters in your story besides the main character. Who are they, and what do they look like?

What are these other characters like? Are they funny, serious, kind, or maybe a little mischievous? Could you describe their personalities?

What are the other characters' favorite activities, foods, or hobbies? How do these preferences show their personalities?

How does Zoe interact with these other characters? Do they get along, have disagreements, or help each other in challenging situations?

How do the other side characters influence the story's events? Are they involved in the central conflict or help solve a big problem?

Side Character Notes or Drawings...

Conflict and Resolution Questions-

What big problems and challenges does Zoe face in the story?

How does Zoe react when she first encounters the central conflict? What emotions or actions does she show?

How are the side characters involved in the central conflict? Do they help or make things more complicated for the main character?

What steps does Zoe take to resolve the conflict? Does she need to make a tough decision or take a significant risk?

Is there an unexpected twist or turn in how the conflict evolves or is resolved? What surprises the characters?

How is the conflict finally resolved? What changes occur in the story because of this resolution?

How do the main and side characters feel about how the conflict was resolved? Are they relieved, happy, sad, or something else?

What important lessons do the characters learn from facing and resolving the conflict? How do these lessons change them?

How does the resolution of the conflict impact the characters and the world of your story in the long run?

How do the characters' relationships change after the conflict is resolved? Do they become closer, or are there new challenges they face?

Conflict and Resolution Notes or Drawings...

Ending Questions-

Could you describe how your story ends? What happens in the final scenes?

Could you describe the setting where the story ends? How is it different from the beginning?

How does Zoe feel at the end of the story? Is she happy, sad, relieved, or something else?

How has Zoe changed from the beginning of the story to the end?

What happens to the side characters at the end of the story? How are their stories wrapped up?

Are any questions or mysteries left unanswered at the end of the story? Why were they left unresolved?

What is the main lesson or message of the story at its conclusion? What do you want your readers to take away?

Ending Notes or Drawings...

Story Notes

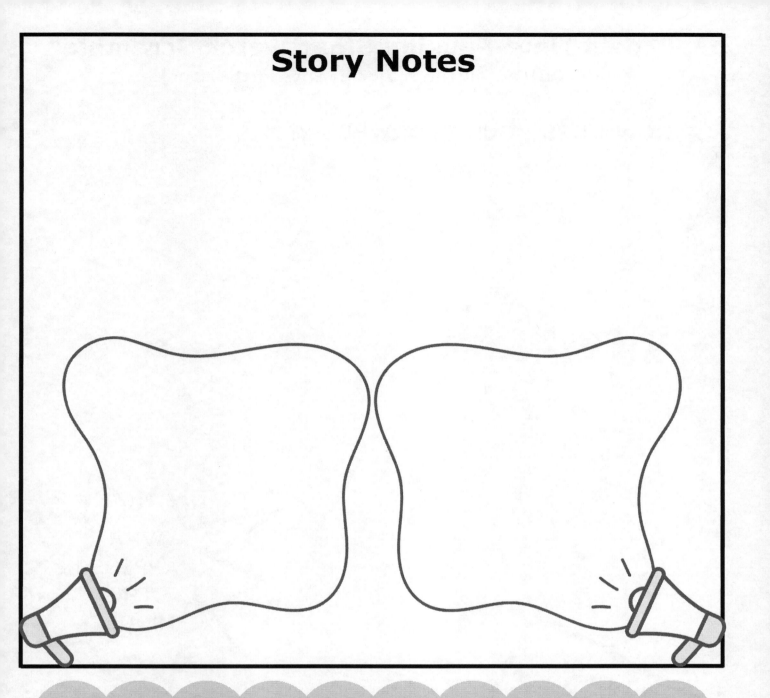

It's time for you to write your own unique story! Before you start, could you outline how your story will go? It helps to outline your story in a beginning, middle, and end. Consider when you will introduce characters, where the story starts and ends, when you introduce your conflict and resolution, etc. Good luck; you are going to do great!

"Zoe's Time-Pausing Smartwatch Scramble"
Outline all the major events in the story

HOW DOES YOUR STORY BEGIN?

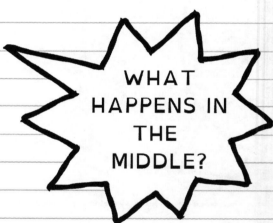
WHAT HAPPENS IN THE MIDDLE?

HOW DOES YOUR STORY END?

"Zoe's Time-Pausing Smartwatch Scramble"

> "THE MORE YOU LIKE YOURSELF, THE LESS YOU ARE LIKE ANYONE ELSE, WHICH MAKES YOU UNIQUE." - WALT DISNEY

"BE YOURSELF; EVERYONE ELSE IS ALREADY TAKEN."

- OSCAR WILDE

"Zoe's Time-Pausing Smartwatch Scramble"

"IF YOU CAN DREAM IT, YOU CAN DO IT."

- WALT DISNEY

"THERE IS POWER IN BEING HOPEFUL AND OPTIMISTIC, EVEN WHEN EVERYTHING SEEMS TO BE FALLING APART."

-AMANDA GORMAN

"Zoe's Time-Pausing Smartwatch Scramble"

"LIFE ISN'T ABOUT WAITING FOR THE STORM TO PASS, IT'S ABOUT LEARNING TO DANCE IN THE RAIN." - VIVIAN GREENE

"SUCCESS IS NOT FINAL, FAILURE IS NOT FATAL: IT IS THE COURAGE TO CONTINUE THAT COUNTS."
- WINSTON CHURCHILL

"Zoe's Time-Pausing Smartwatch Scramble"

"TWENTY YEARS FROM NOW YOU WILL BE MORE DISAPPOINTED BY THE THINGS YOU DIDN'T DO THAN BY THE ONES YOU DID DO." - MARK TWAIN

IF YOU ENJOYED THIS SCIENCE FICTION PROMPT, YOU WILL LOVE THIS BOOK WITH 6 UNIQUE SCIFI PROMPTS

NEED MORE SPACE TO WRITE? GRAB AN EMPTY NOTEBOOK OR CHECK OUT THIS KEEPSAKE JOURNAL!

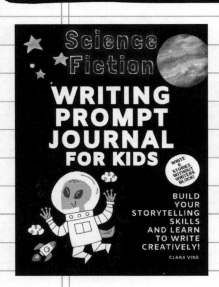

UNLOCK YOUR PHONE AND USE THE CAMERA FOR LINK!

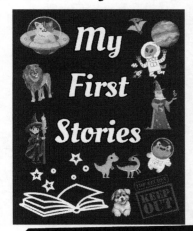

CHAPTER 10

What Did You Learn?

Congratulations, you have written six unique stories! It is time to reflect on what you have learned and created in this book.

What have you learned about storytelling and creativity from these writing prompts?

If you were to rewrite one of your stories, what would you do differently this time?

Do you feel like your writing skills were improved? If so, how?

Which story you wrote was your favorite, and why does it stand out?

What character was your favorite to write about and why?

How does writing make you feel? It can be more than one emotion!

CHAPTER 11

Glossary

Glossary

Atmosphere: The feeling or mood of a place. For example, a birthday party has a happy atmosphere.

Cozy: Very comfortable and warm, like snuggling up in a soft blanket.

Detaches: Separates or comes apart from something.

Echolocate: To find things by making sounds and listening to the echoes.

Ecosystem: All the living things in an area and how they interact with each other and their environment.

Elements: Different parts or pieces of something. In a story, elements could be things like magic, adventure, or friendship.

Enchanted: Something that has been given magical powers or is under a spell.

Environment: The area around you, including things like trees, buildings, and the weather.

Essence: The most important qualities or characteristics of something.

Exploration: Going to new places and learning about them.

Fantasy: A kind of story with magic and things that don't exist in the real world.

Finite: Having a limit or end.

Hiccups: Small, involuntary movements of the diaphragm that cause a sudden intake of breath.

Inhabitants: The people or creatures that live in a place.

Intricate: Having many small parts or details that are arranged in a complicated way.

Invisible: Unable to be seen.

Landmarks: Special places that are easy to recognize and remember, like a big statue or a famous building.

Glossary Continued

Magical realm: A make-believe world where magic exists and anything is possible.

Mild: Not too hot and not too cold; just right.

Misjudged: Formed a wrong opinion or made an incorrect judgment about someone or something.

Mischievous: Playful in a naughty or annoying way.

Portal: A magical doorway that can take you to another place.

Potion: A magical liquid with special powers.

Ragtag: A group of people or things that are disorganized, unkempt, or not put together well. For example, you might describe a marching band as ragtag if they have mismatched outfits and a variety of instruments. You might also describe a team as ragtag if it's poorly organized and not respectable.

Realm: Another word for a world or kingdom, especially in stories with magic.

Sinister: Giving the impression that something harmful or evil is happening or will happen.

Sorcerer: A person who can use magic, similar to a wizard.

Timeless: Something that doesn't belong to any specific time period and could fit in many different times.

Tranquil: Calm and peaceful.

Vibrant: Full of energy and enthusiasm.

Vivid: Very bright, clear, and colorful.

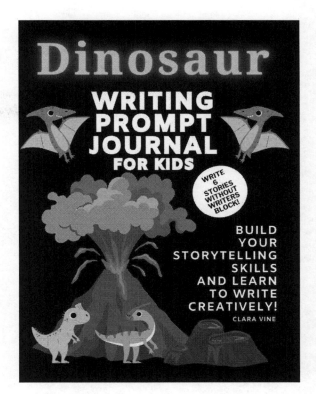

UNLOCK YOUR PHONE AND OPEN THE CAMERA FOR THE LINK!

Made in the USA
Columbia, SC
20 December 2024

50139167R00104